To Hope

AF623659

Minela Hadzic

BookLeaf Publishing

Presentation by *BookLeaf Publishing*

Web: www.bookleafpub.com

E-mail: info@bookleafpub.com

ISBN: 9789357441759

First edition 2023

DEDICATION

To a place where the sun rises and the moon never sleeps.

To anyone who has loved and lost.

To my younger self, who I fought very hard to find, who began a journey to look for her treasure only to lose herself. To her beloved who is no longer here.

I've spent years writing about her, writing to her and if she ever gets lost again I hope this will keep her grounded and remind her of her purpose and allow her to feel the pain she ran from, in order to heal.

Constant battle with PTSD/BPD, a collection of poems written during hard times.

ACKNOWLEDGEMENT

Praise and Thanks be to God for showing me the way and not giving up on me, for I now realise everything happens for a reason and my burdens are for me to carry.

To all the professional help for my Ptsd/Bpd and Graves Disease and constant reminders for when I forget myself, Thank you.

For all those I love and have loved. Thank you for being patient with me.

To those who have hurt me, Thank you, am still trying, growing, glowing.

To My favourite people, the writers, the dreamers, the misfits. You are my inspiration.

Thanks to James Arthur, for his music saved me on so many occasions, especially titles - Certain Things, Maybe. Sermon, Hurts, You. Underrated Artist.

To S. Gomez with "Lose you to love me" and most importantly for standing up for Mental Health. I appreciate it.

To everyone who is struggling to find a purpose, I hope you find it soon.

PREFACE

“Remember that wherever your heart is, there you will find your treasure.”
- P.Coelho

An excerpt from my book 'Romeo and Majnoon'. I haven't yet published it but 'the bench' plays a big part in this collection too.

"Sometimes I watched her from a distance, I knew she wasn't there, where she sat at that very moment. Once, she told me, her favourite place was a bench in a park. She took the train on Thursdays just to sit there, overwhelmed, she cried.

At that moment in time, I didn't understand why someone would go through so much grief and pain, just to be reminded of where she sat, next to him.

"It's the only place I feel him", she said.

I guessed that's a memory she wants to keep, the conversation she had last had with him was at that very place and the only time, in a decade where she believed he was being honest.
Maybe she lied to herself but, I could tell this girl needed this pain to feel alive again. I have never met anyone more in love with a man she never had or will never have, he must have been so important to her, for her whole life was shaped by this 'Love'.

I came to the conclusion that, he must have taken so much away from her, that she lost herself completely and the only way to find her again was to feel close to him. So she sits there, still, motionless as her eyes wonder and her heart recalling the memories that have the missing pieces of who she once was. I cried too in the end, I knew I would never experience such a thing, no two loves are the same. I wondered whether I was envious of her, wanting for just a moment, to feel the love she feels.

Cold 92'

In the distance cold
there's truth to be told.
I will not whisper, will not slide
I"ll scream, not let the truth hide

Weeping willows shedding tears
stand tall in a row
soaked up with past fears
bent precisely in a bow.

Deserted life on blooded streets
time and time again
people hushed with silence hurt
wounds washed in the rain.

Shaky voices on the radio
walking sticks and fears
people walking with a cracked smile
hiding all hearts tears.

Time has come once again
for the truth to come out
Justice fled in split seconds
like air we can't live without.

The wait of silenced hills has come
the shaking trees in the skies
only at night when the birds are sleeping
can you hear all the cries?

Lost souls in the washed-up soil
scattered here and there
nameless bodies found again
life, was never fair.

Gunshots like irritating flies,
fill the air with smoke.
I remember this like yesterday
and how the silence broke.

Smell of flesh and naked trees,
the world in black and gray
A silent tear and a hopeless wish
A dream in a war's day.

Constant yelling and sad cries
from corners of each room.
The countdown to each one dead
Too young, old and - soon!

A maze of mines and bullet shells,
were two of many games.
Suffering and blooded smells,
bodies without names.

A walking stick, an old smoke pipe
left there on the floor.
The old man's hands above his head
and words of 'Please no more'.

A baby's cot, two blue bears
hugging in the snow.
A mother's sobs without her child
who she'll never see grown.

A fellow neighbour's secret smile,
a hand from a friend,
Weeping willows in the river,
a fright which has no end.

Hardened footsteps,
Heavy blows and a bullet in the head,
is what I felt when I first died,
at the age of 8.

Memories and happy turns,
God Almighty's love
has left the heart to beat again
and carry 'hope' above.

Sky

Sky, a magical canvas speckled with star-light.
Endlessly, I stare and think.
I whisper my wishes to the misbehaving wind..
Afraid I'll miss it if I blink.

I breathe in my last thought, as I feel the ripples in the well of my eyes.
I smile, to my own surprise.

I close my eyes, as dreamers do.
I wait for the effect.
...and there my heartbeat spells the name of who I least expect.

So may the wind go high above the crown on that moon... Tonight my only wish.. Is to see you, soon.

Rain

She taps on my window.
Tap. Tap. Tap.
Quietly, but suddenly.

Announcing her fury, her agitation.
Every single drop racing with my own.
Hers from the sky and mine from the ocean.
Ocean in my eyes.

My heart beats in duet with each tap.
I'm hurting, then....

P e a c e.

Like nothing happened, each drop full of emotion,
that only today will witness, tomorrow never will.

Predictable, but after each one of her visits ....
The S u n.

Like a smile,
hugging my face with its warmth.

Slowly the Rain vanishes as always does, just as she came,
Instant and uncalled.
So long, until the moment she knows,
I need her again,

Predictable.

Usual.

Consistent.

Blessed Rain,
My best friend...
always there so I don't fall alone.

Paper Hearts

I knelt down by the River today,
had to tell it a secret,
I knew it would flow into
the sea, that knew how to keep it.

Emptied my pockets of imaginary hearts,
and picked up a pebble or two.
Just to throw them back in the river again,
Imagining the river was you.

The river knew the message it carried,
And I think that was enough,
and I guess it knew from the pebbles I threw in, that I
wasn't all that tough.

But I did walk away with a smile,
For In my heart I knew,
The raging storm at sea that day,
Will be a reflection of you.

Uninvited

Invader of dreams,
master of seduction.
Leader of the path,
to one's self-destruction.

Aware of my smile,
I lay still, consumed.
Toxic flowing in my veins
He remains amused.

Often I have wondered,
how I would (truly) feel?!
If I had just imagined it

had it not been real.

I know better now,
time has served me well.
leading me to rise,
where I always fell.

Heartbeat intermittent,
a twist in my gut.
A Well begins to over-spill,
my eyes finally shut.

Exhale all the sorrow, the grief
and endless pain.
Echo from my heart,
Never again! Never again! Never again.

I lock away dreams,
Wave to the starry sky.
Throw away the key,
and whisper my goodbye.

Nothing is as it seems,
something I know best.
"looks can be deceiving", He said.
So I lay that ghost to rest.

I see clearly now,
I guess, in the end.
What we think is living,
Is just walking dead.

The twisting of my gut,
Stabbing in my heart.
Was never a kind of love,
but a pain from the start.

I could write another line.
To tell you how I feel,
but I figure it best to save my words,
for something that feels real.

Too Close, Too Far

(240 months ago)

Even though the sun is millions of miles away,
I can still feel it on my face.

Though, the stars hang from the skies,
You could still see them in my eyes.

If I sank to the bottom of the ocean,
You would recognise my devotion.

And if time separated us for a while,
I would see me in your smile.

And when Angels are near me,
I still feel your presence.

But, when you are near,
You are never quite, here.

1 foot, 2 feet, 3 feet or 6
Like the meeting of the two seas that never mix.

When death takes me away,
I will be in the beat of your heart.

So close, yet so far
I'll be waiting on the other side,

Where our souls finally meet
and our hearts can touch.

(Before you go to sleep tonight, think of me)

Tattoo

Staring in the mirror,
a pain within.
Before me,
the wings of my sin.

My face,
a permanent frown,
Pen in my hand,
I look down.

Ink all over my fingertips,
the pen, like my heart, begins to drip.
I clench my fists, as tears fall
down my face and onto my lips.

Here, I remember it all.
Pictures of Butterflies on these walls.

I know what I'm doing, no mistake
Soon, the pen in my hand will break,
Heart thumping, mind insane,
My eyes strolling down memory lane.

My chest, now a faster pace
as my whole life, slides down my face.
In front, myself, as clear as can be.
I now see the old me.

No room for thoughts nor regrets,
Walls, it smells, of stale cigarettes.
The strangest man I had ever seen,
Tattoos, a beard and dressed in green.

He moves closer slow and steady,
he mumbles the words 'are you ready?'
Through his hairy lips he continues to talk,

as my mind decides to walk.

Again I go back I feel afraid,
Things I wanted but never made.
I remember your words, I begin to cry
Because I was your,
Butterfly.

I felt your lips as you placed your kiss,
Am I really doing this?
The man awaits to begin the trace,
in that exact, same place.

The needle, the buzz and the pain on my skin.
is nothing compared to the hurt within.
I remember you again, and take a deep breath in,
and whisper 'ready' for him to begin.

Back again looking in the mirror,
my sin now, looks even bigger.
Permanent souvenir of my insanity.
Because I am me, a walking travesty.

Favourite things

I don't need, what everyone needs,
or want, what everyone wants,
I am happy with a little sun,
a field,
wildflowers that grow from stones,
peace and quiet.
Chirping birds,
sound of a river or waterfalls
stillness of the moment.
Sound of children laughing.
My favourite songs,
Blessed Rain
Smell of snow.
Fluffy animals

Kind hearts,
Empathy
I don't, dream of 'things' like,
cars, luxuries or bloody money.
I dream of lands, far away,
Pomegranates, milk and honey.
Oranges, fig trees and olives
Mountain tops
Counting on my fingers x33

Of bees,
The face of the Moon
The stars.
Waving to clouds.
Hugging a tree.
Weeping willows.
Snowdrops
Autumn fallen leaves.
Not chasing likes and hits,
Or any of your man-made bits.
Dewdrops
Love, for the sake of God
Wise words,
Smell of books,
A cedar candle
Macorons (Almonds)
Herbal teas
A cup of morning coffee.
My heart content
A clear conscience
Clock strikes 12'
Praying at Midnight.
Some understanding,

I don’t quite know how am still standing.

These are a few of 'my favourite things.'

Souls

Soul

'"Eyes are the window to the soul", he said.
It was only when he looked at me,
I could hear my own heart beat.
Little did he know, how much of me belonged to him
at that moment.
More than I belonged to myself,
and the more he looked into my eyes,
the less I owned my soul.

Some souls recognise each other,
because they have already met somewhere, they had
a meeting before they even saw each other.
Same as you and same as me but,
not you, and me.

No, we've never met before, we never saw each other,
heard each other or looked into the eyes of one
another.
I don't know you.
You don't know me.

I just feel you, somewhere between where the soul
begins and the heart stops.
That's a gift from God.

No, I don't need you close to me,
nor do I pray that you are but,
the soul dies every night, a short death and when it returns, it still knows you.
So far, yet so close.

but, I don't know you and that's absolutely fine.

Dear Stranger,

Shaking, as I write these words,
Tightly holding my pen.
Beside me a letter with no names,
Dated Friday, 31 December 2010.

It might have been November,
Forgive me, my memory is not strong.
I began reading it,
and everything went wrong.

You see, the thing is,
The strangest thing of all,
The old letter is written by me,
but I don't remember at all.

I can't recall much thereafter,
or what the letter said.
You see, there were too many demons,
I thought that I was dead.

It was all too quick for me,
I must have hit my head,
and all that I remember from it all is,
waking up in a hospital bed.

In all the confusion, as time went by,
All I could do was pray.
I believed if I get closer to God,
He would show me the way.

I prayed hard, still confused
fighting with all might,
The meds, the demons, the voices
The struggles, I had to fight.

Alone and confused,
Changing meds, another November by then,
It crossed my mind but, I refused
and it was then, when...

I saw you, Stranger
Just down the road, little round about,
Looking at me from a distance,
as I tried to work it out.

It was only a minute, you stood still,
Distorted but, I could see,
While losing my balance I stared back
as you stared at me.

Since that day,
I don't know, How? I remembered you.
If I'm wrong and you don't know me,
then, none of this is true.

It's been 9 months and 11 days,
Since you looked at me,
and all the years leading to now,
I have failed to see.

For, I've been forgetful, past few days,
I am losing my way
but I decided to read the letter,
to see what it had to say.

Opening the shoe box, the letter,
Though I don't know who it's for,
I wonder what it meant to say,
Exactly 12 years ago.

Dream

"Sometimes you have to travel a long way to find what is near."
-P. Coelho

Climbed the mountains,
Asked the 7 seas,
Spoke to all the animals,
And talked to the trees.

I even Asked the sun, stars and the moon
"Do you know where my treasure is?"
they said,
"Pray!
and you shall find it soon."

One night I was praying,
then I fell asleep,
A dream occurred, I woke up
and began to weep.

The dream was very short,
hard to understand.
A man stood before me,
and took me by the hand.

He said gently, "Hello there."
I felt such a pleasure,
"I know it's been a while, but
Now let's find your treasure".

For the first time in years,
I could feel my heart,
beating in its place finally
but that was just a start.

I longed to have a dream again,
to see this perfect stranger,
Meanwhile in reality,
My life was in danger.

By now I was in Love,
With a man I never met.
Perfect stranger, with the gentle voice
I just can't forget.

One night In Winter I dreamt,
Me as a young girl,
and A boy about the same age,
and I was holding a pearl.

We were on a beach,
barefoot in the sand
everything around us feeling just right.
Holding hands and laughing,
both dressed in white.
I will never forget, that cold winter night.

Shoebox

I never owned an expensive pair of shoes and most
certainly not the shoes, that came in this box.

It wasn't even my box.

It was just, thrown out,
Outside the old apartment by a skip.

I saved it from the rain,
I put in it all my nothings,

and when I moved back home, it remained,
unopened, undisturbed.
Out of sight, collecting decade-full of dust.

but, when I opened it again to really have a look, It
contained the following:

One train ticket, for a trip up north dated Oct 2008

A silver, empty cigarette box of 10 with a cinema
ticket tucked inside.

Gum wrappers- Airways, blackcurrant

A small glass Butterfly, blue, remains of broken
windchimes.

A pen without ink, without a lid.

A4 poster of the meaning of my name and underneath, a 6-digit number.

A small piece of paper with a list of songs on it in this precise order.

Unwritten - N.Bedingfield.
Gotta get thru this - D. Bedingfield.
Hero - E.Eglesias.
Da Sutis- D. Merlin.
Tera Mera Pyar - K.Sanu.
Undo - D.Merlin
Moja Srno-D. Polumenta.
Ko zna gdje si ove noci-D. Polumenta.
Rane-D.Merlin.

Empty perfume bottle and a pearl inside it.

and the letter dated 2010.

Letter 2010

Dear, (letter 2010)

Thank you, for the past month, please don't think I'll forget, for the letter you wrote to my mother, of all your past regrets.
Thank you for the times of happiness, it only lasted a while, for driving a hundred miles, just to make me smile.
I know that you wanted, for me to just come back, but the day you turned away from me everything went black.

My life is difficult here, reminds me of us, the days you played behind me I lost all my trust.
It's okay, you're moving on in search of happiness, this is on me now to clean up my own mess.

All I can say is from this day on, I know that am alone, you took my heart and soul with you and you and I, we're done. There's just so much left unsaid, I don't think it's fair, So I'm writing you this letter with all I want to say.

Dear honey, I'm sitting on the bench we sat, just the other day, recalling past memories and all you had to say.
Vicky Park empty today, not many people around, just myself and a few pigeons and not too many sounds.

Anyway the other day, you were talking about Joy, "She was always in the picture". You said, and I felt like a toy.
"You won't do the same to her, will you?", I asked, you thought for a while then said "No!", forgetting all our past.

Feeling alone in the world, though it's probably what I deserve, I don't think things will get better, maybe one day when you read this letter.
For now I'll sit here feeling blue, I choose this bench for when I think of you.

When you left the other day, I took out of my locket, a pearl, as you put your shoes on, I placed it in your pocket. I hope you will find it and no one else will see, I'm hoping when you do, that you'll think of me. I wish it was something bigger, I hope you don't mind it, but then again I didn't tell you and you might not even find it.

I won't forget our kisses, the taste of blackcurrant and the smell of my own perfume mixed with your 'touch', the 'only red' sweets you picked, coz' they were my favourite, am sad coz' all I gave you was a stupid bracelet.

Before you start a life without me, don't forget, me, maybe I will do the same but only God can see. Maybe I find love somewhere, just can't see it now, a couple of kids before I'm gray, I just can't see how.

I just don't feel worthy right now, of happiness, of love. Oh, it's started raining, I love the rain, but my letter is wet and I just have to go. Just got home and forgot about the time, my kitten is at the door he heard the wind chimes.

Easy tiger, am back again and it's 4 am, while the world is sleeping, you know how strange I am. Anyway, I'm writing, I have so much to say. Things I couldn't say the day you drove away.

I'm sorry you think I hurt you and broke your heart, that's the reason I went away to make a fresh new start, but he really hurt me, I love you and you know it's true. I tried to call you that day, I just couldn't get through. I'll never forget the pain that day and your number ending 762.

I will write to you for years to come, this I promise you, I thought of writing songs to sell to dedicate to you.
I know, it's stupid I have a job, but it's something I want to do, you might come across a song one day and think "I know that's you."

I may write some lyrics, honestly, sell all my words, if it does happen just remember they're all about me and you. Before I go you must know this, for 'just in case', I love you! this is my oath and no one will take your place.

When you're old, you ever find yourself, alone or feeling blue, hold the pearl and remember me, when I was a silly girl.
Come find me one day, just don't treat me like a toy.
Forgive if I ever hurt you, I hope you find joy in Joy.

I don't know how to give you this letter, I'm just under so much stress. I think I'll come up North next week, wait, you gave me an address. You gave it to me, to where I can send my book, I just can't find it and don't know where to look.

I can't believe it, heard the news, you had an accident, you died peacefully in a foreign town and I, wasn't there. To hold you my dear, to say I love you, still can't believe that it, is true. That's it, that's me done am not living without you.

Dear Honey, I know you're there, I still see you in my dreams, they just hurt when I wake up because I know it's not real.
I know you are near, watching over me, as I read this book, about a boy in search of his treasure, I'm crying, but look.

I've packed my things, moving back home but I won't see you around. I promise to pray for you, maybe I too have a treasure and I know how this might sound. I have nothing else left in the world, I don’t know who I am, you were the only one who really loved me when no one gave a damn.

Panic attack

It starts suddenly, first in my chest.
Then my palms feel hot, they start to sweat.
My shoulders are heavy and so are my arms.
Palpitations and pounding around my heart.

No warning at all, my heart in my throat.
I start to count 10 to zero
Oh, can they hear me? Am I saying it quietly
Are they looking behind me or straight through my head?

I can't stand here, need to escape
Not feeling secure not feeling safe.
Should I back out or just walk through
Oh just leave the shopping and walk out of the queue.

I hear them all at once
The sound of the trolleys and the wheels and tills
It's all just too close to my ears.
Keep walking straight through the crowd, I need a wee and everything's so loud.

Grab a cab, breathing too heavy
The motion now makes me feel sick
I open the window, think I'll throw up
"Nice day today" someone says.

Am now neither here nor there
the cars moving fast but slow
All distorted images
Smoke, rain, bloody flashbacks.

I'm in a forest, then back in the car
Everything close to me now looks so far
I can feel the tears, I know am crying
Shall I try and smile and at
the same time I am dying.

Something is about to happen
I feel it, can't shake it off
I can't really explain it to the driver
He's looking on, I don't feel safe.

I feel my veins,
The throbbing of my blood
The cab man now thinks, I'm just rude.
but I'm not, I remain quiet I'd explain if I could.

I run out quickly, say "keep the change"
I need to run home, need to escape.
I feel a knife in my chest, just need to get in, need to
get home.

Breathing too quick, key in the door
Bring myself slowly to sit on the floor
Looking around to see where I am
And start to count again and again.

I look around to see what's near me
54321 a table, a vase, beautiful flowers, a window and my TV.
I smell my perfume and fabric conditioner, I start to feel a little easier.

I can hear the dryer from the corner of the room, it's ok, am inside, I am safe and I am home. I begin to feel like an idiot, nothing will happen and nothing to worry about.

Being me

“They don’t know better. I usually just smile and let it slide. Maybe someday they’ll get it, though for their sake, I usually hope not.” — Unknown

"Today's a good day, a good day" I say.
but the pain still lingers within
I need to stop it I'm going insane
It's in my veins, under my skin.

Head all jumbled and sometimes not there, maybe I'll read or play a game,
maybe a bath, a candle, my journal
Or maybe just let it be.

I try my best to be normal and when I am things are okay.
It lasts a while but then again
am back at the first square.

Feel so tired, so exhausted
I didn't get much sleep last night.
The meds help, I do try, wait that's a lie
I haven't slept much in 30 years.

Lights are on, I'm not scared
I really have no fear,
just random something sets me off
then, it’s war, right now - right here.

Don't know what's more confusing,
My head or the Graves disease, blood tests,
appointments.
So many times, days and dates
Shit! I've written it all somewhere but don’t
remember where.

Shattered, just can’t move
I need a shower and some rest, but I just have so
much to do
It will just have to wait.
Still standing, don’t know how?
It’s 3 am, am awake
Nightmares, stress and thoughts again
..and back to sleep.

Today’s a good day, the meds are working, I feel
well.
Though my body still feels like it's just been through
hell.
I look zombie-like, pale and green but,
Make-up, can anyone even tell?

I'm doing my best, my very best
What others say I don’t give a sh..
Not anymore because, this is me
It's what I am it's how I live.

I'm a shell, an empty shell
Days are hard but, nights as well
Sometimes 3 and sometimes 4
I keep going but very slow.
I know it won't be forever,
just need to put myself back together.

I tell my other self, hey give-me-five
You got this, you will survive
You can do this, you did it before
and look at you now you came back stronger, No!
This is not the end.

I know you're trying, it's okay to cry,
You're allowed and you still stand out from the crowd. You're worthy of life and you've a lot to be grateful for, just remember that.

Our little pep talk, just me and I, literally.

I wonder what they think or if they would survive,
just living one day like me in my life.

Me

You can't put me down,
the way I can lift you up.
You can throw me, slap me, downgrade me.
Attempt to destroy me, curse me slate me.
Go ahead of course, you can even hate me.

But

You can't kill my faith, my heart
my soul, nor change me.
For nothing is stronger nor greater,
than The One who made me.

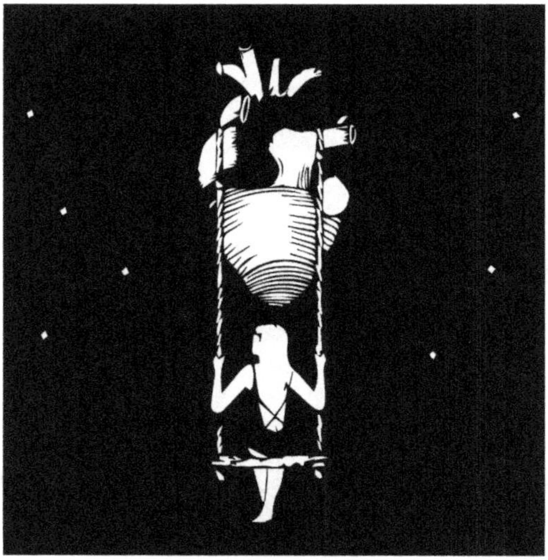

Kintsugi

"Kintsugi [is] not just a method of repair but also a philosophy. It's the belief that the breaks, cracks, and repairs become a valuable and esteemed part of the history of an object, rather than something to be hidden. That, in fact, the piece is more beautiful for having been broken."
-Kathleen Tessaro

My body is like a perfectly broken ornament made
somewhere in Japan.

I imagine how easy it was to break this time, each
painful piece carrying its own. Like the earth when it
quakes, deep scars, cracks.
Although we can't reach within, at least we try.

There, we paint our own scars, kintsugi-style, gold,
glistening and shiny gold lines. Embracing the pain
and letting go all at the same time, then become even
more beautiful than before.

Life, a breaker, but you can choose to remain broken
or to heal, to become stronger, more resilient and
flawless amidst all its flaws after breaking.

Feel the scars, become as unique as you are for no two pains are ever the same and shine.
Shine like the gold of your scars.

My Lord

"O Lord, the stars are shining, and the eyes are
sleeping,
The kings have shut their doors.
Each lover is alone with his beloved.
And I am alone with You."

- Rabia Al-Adawiyya

I turn my heart to you my beloved,
fill my heart with your love, only.
Shed away all that's in the way my Lord, like leaves
in autumn when they fall. In with the new, out with
the old.

So when I look around me, all that is left, is what
reminds me of you, only.
Then I know for sure my heart is at peace and my
soul is home.

For my heart, my Lord has been absent and time and
time has passed by. It's been lost for far too long, now
it's peaceful I could cry.

This journey has served me well,
but soon it will be over.
Am grateful, happy and peaceful,
My heart now, with its rightful owner.

And if they took everything away,
now that I have grown,
I know it will be what you decree
You, My Lord, King of the throne.

O My Master, bestow your mercy,
and forgiveness on my soul.
Bless me with patience and strength,
My Lord, please answer my call.

Amin.

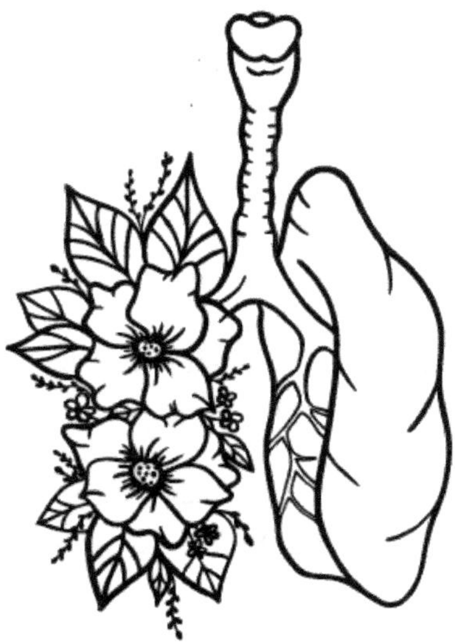

The Pearl

I carried a pearl in my locket,
for so so many years,
it brought with it memories,
of laughter and many tears.

The one true thing I remember,
It brought me closer to God.
It was my reminder,
for if I ever gotten lost.

Given to me by someone special,
along with a crown for my head,
A Holy book and some beads,
to pray before I'm dead.

I'd forgotten the Holy book,
when I took off my Crown,
I gave the pearl away one day
and that's how it all went down.

It took a long time to find it,
and when I finally did.
It reminded me of The book,
The crown and what it hid.

For when I lost the one pearl,
It didn't cross my mind,
when I finally open The Book,
how many more I'd find.

So I'm sitting here overwhelmed,
with Pearls in my hands,
reflecting on what it took
Only God understands.

To get here, to be able to smile
To finally have found 'Hope'
and hold on tight and never let go,
Of God Almighty's rope.

Now, to the owner of my pearl.
Whilst you're watching over me.
I hope it leads towards Heaven
Where we're both finally free.

I know

I know you feel me talking to you, through the air,
the wind, the mind.

Heart to heart, the slightest thought brings me back to
you.

How did you expect I would fly?
One can only do so much trying before giving up.

Then there is you, the little anonymous sign. I don’t
know if you're building me or killing me but, you're
not letting me go that's for sure.

No matter where we are, like now
So close yet so - far!
Our hearts will always be searching for one another
in the crowds. For peace, for a piece.

Besides, it's only the one who gave you the wings
that can fix them and I don’t know How?! I don’t
know why?!
I need you, to put me back together.

If you ever see me, look away, for everyone's sake. Too much is at stake because I just know, I know, if I look into your eyes?! The Earth will cave in and the skies will open. I know and so do you.

It's Goodbye for now

I ran out of inspiration, so I looked out the window. I saw a squirrel, a cat, a few birds ahead. There are no coincidences.

Sound of the airplane deep in the sky and a few cars drove by.
I thought for a while, thinking how sad my poems have become.

I used to write songs in the snow, up in the mountains covered in white blankets. Feeling cold, blowing warmth into my hands until I can finally sit down open my notepad and lift a pen. Sip on rum and tea, eat the local bread and cheese with grapes and have a cup of coffee or ten in the evening, evenings are my time to write. I lift the pen closest to me and...

As you can probably tell, but I used to write sitting by the river, watching the ripples and throw crumbs in for the fish. Talk to myself a little and change positions.

I walked to castles and over every bridge I could find, looking for that treasure.
I wrote on planes thousands of feet in the skies and nothing ever came close and if it did it was soon snatched right before my eyes. I'd see it published the Tuesday after and I hate Tuesdays.

I'd think that idea was mine but then again who to blame but myself.

I hate Tuesdays because, it's never a good day since I can remember but so be it. I'd lift my pen on the rooftops and sing songs out of tune because I may connect the words well sometimes but can't sing to save my life. I know who will laugh here, wink.

The Alps must be frosty right now, I heard there isn't enough snow, perhaps it's time to reveal a little earth so it can grow a new, more beautiful, resilient layer. The last time there was a shoot, cheer, a lot of tears and a few songs for the heart. I shall carry that with me as I move along, Thank you! For the Guitar, for the words and for the smiles.

I get writer's block and when I do, I randomly write, write and write until something comes to mind. Like an awakening. Then I'd take the closest book to me open page 54 and read line 16 just for fun to see if I'm meant to find some sort of message from the universe, just for me.

The biggest miracle came to me when I found God or he found me, I'm not sure this time because I'd hit rock bottom and they say "Pray, maybe you were supposed to find something down there"
Then I realised, I'm not close to God on top of Mountains, nor rooftops nor when I'm in the depths of the sky.
I was closest when my head touched the ground, and there, right at the bottom is where I finally found it.

My treasure,

I always thought my treasure was my heart. It is but, it was what was in my heart in the very first place before it got replaced by someone who probably means nothing now, I wouldn't know because I don't remember. Amnesic isn't always that bad, the phases are a little scary but do wonders for things or people you shouldn't even remember.

Anyway, I found the pearl. I found my heart and I found God.
When I found God he led me to my purpose again and I think I can finally breathe again, hear again and see again. I don't know for how long but il keep on keeping strong.

Yes, so I get writer's block often. I usually list down all my wishes, places I'd like to go and see, things I haven't done yet and there aren't that many, perhaps my imagination isn't all that up to scratch as it used to be and am not as adventurous, then again health.

This year will be different, this year il be collecting moments with those close to me, it is the moments I now live for, not things, well, maybe a few more notebooks and a couple of pens.

I may complete the book I've yet to publish before I die, one day this year perhaps. Maybe it's time to spread my wings and fly, finally.

Ah, just got an idea for my new poem. See this is how writer's block works. I will just ignore it, write as random as possible and find something that rhymes.

The story of two wolves was inspiring, but suppose everyone knows that.
I did come across a poem, it didn’t rhyme either, but it was about a girl as 'little red riding hood' who ate all the apples through the forest but still hungry and then came across a wolf and looked him dead in the eye and said " I could gobble you up" so the wolf fled obviously, happy her anti-depressants worked. Mine works a little differently, but it was a great poem about appetite.

I was going to write about the story of the 'Prince and the flower seeds' but figured there’s nothing more to add, the moral is there and why would I do anything with that seeing as it's my favourite story and I’ll keep it as it is in my mind. When I first read it, I think I cried as it really moved me.

I could write about the seasons but they're all in my book, I could describe how amazing sand looks under a microscope, have you seen it? Gems is the word. It's the little random things that make me smile and steal my heart nowadays, if you're normal, you're not my cup of tea. "If you were everyone's cup of tea then you'd be a mug" I read that somewhere too.

When the clock strikes midnight I'm usually engaged in a prayer, then I whisper 'I love you' and usually I don't direct this to anyone in particular but, I have done this for decades every single night without fail.

I don't like goodbyes, I think this is what I am trying to say here. I think we will meet again, perhaps in one of my books, maybe even in a song or 2 yet to come, wink. I really can't sing, for those who know this did I say 'I love you'? Well, I am now. I owe you for the opportunity to express, to unload and you have been an amazing company throughout the years.

I remember years ago someone said 'You are going to make it big one day' I still don't understand what they meant but I'm guessing 'known' and that's the last thing I want however, I'd like to make someone smile and that for me is bigger than anything.

I still can't bring myself to an end, I guess it's time to take the plasters off of my heart, to take back my key. Time to spread these wings, kintsugi-style, wink. Time to close this very dark and long chapter, it's certainly been a long ride. I know there will be things I'll slowly forget again but, should I publish this one day it will help me to remember who I was. I think I'm finally done speaking, for now.

None of this rhymes I realise now.

www.ingramcontent.com/pod-product-compliance
Lightning Source LLC
Chambersburg PA
CBHW051736130826
49812CB00033B/883
9789357441759